BUILDING LANGUAGE

Michael Clay Thompson

Royal Fireworks Press

Copyright @ 2003, Royal Fireworks Publishing Company, Inc.
All Rights Reserved — All Copying Prohibited
Royal Fireworks Publishing Company
First Avenue, P.O. Box 399
Unionville, NY 10988
845 726-4444
FAX 845 726-3824
Email rfpress@frontiernet.net
ISBN: 0-88092-584-1 Student Book / 0-88092-585-X Teacher Manual
Printed in the United States of America
on acid-free paper using vegetable-based inks
by the Royal Fireworks Printing Company
of Unionville, New York.

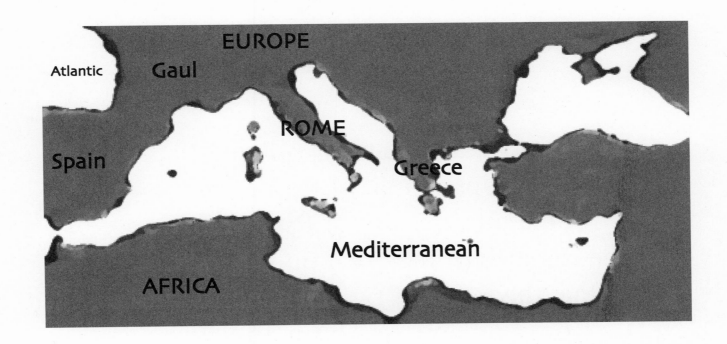

ROME, ROCKS, WORDS

Two thousand years ago,
before Europeans discovered
the back of the world and its people,
ancient Rome ruled the lands
surrounding the Mediterranean Sea.

✎ First, a historical discussion that provides a basis for our vocabulary study. Talk with students about how the New World was the undiscovered back of the world, from the European point of view. Use a globe!

Today, the ruins of the
ancient capital of Rome are
in the modern city of Rome, Italy,
and the remains of the great buildings and roads
that the Romans built can be found
from England, to Africa, to Spain.

Let the students find Italy on the previous page.

Italy is shaped like a boot.

✎ This is a good time for a brief geography lesson, showing students Italy's relationship to other places in the world.

The arches are often the last parts standing.

In these silent ruins, we still see one of Rome's greatest gifts to human civilization, the **arch**.

✎ Point out the arches among these ruins. Have students think about the long time that has passed as these buildings have fallen into ruin.

THE ARCH

The **arch**, with its graceful curve
of hand-shaped stones,
gave Roman buildings
strength and beauty,
and was so important
to ancient construction that even today,
the science of building
structures is called **arch**itecture.

✎ The aesthetic side
of knowledge is very
important. Emphasize
the beauty of the arch.
Often, perfect forms
are beautiful.

At the center of the arch is the **keystone**, shaped to send the weight and force of the arch down to the ground below.

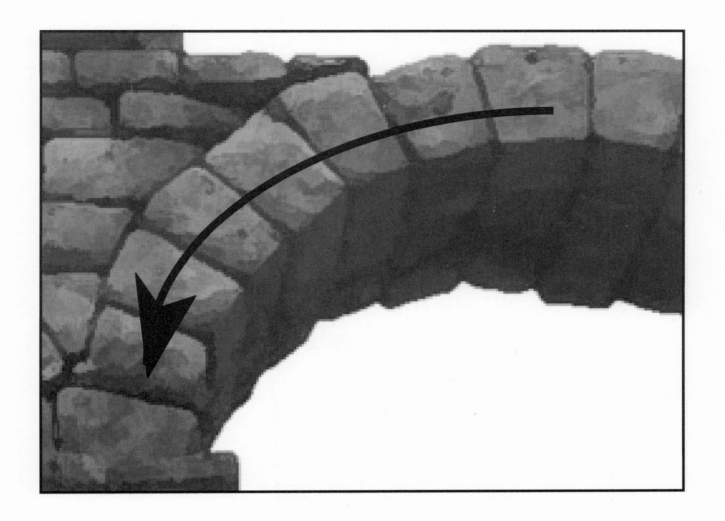

The arch shifts the weight
to the columns on either side.

✎ Have students look carefully at how each stone is shaped, so that the stones rest against each other perfectly.

AQUEDUCTS

Romans used rows of arches,
one on top of another,
to make **aqueducts**,
which carried cold, fresh water
from the mountains down to the city.
In the aqueduct at Segovia, Spain,
there is no cement;
the arches are so strong
that the aqueduct still stands.

✎ The water flowed down a channel built into the top of the aqueduct. The angle of descent had to be just right, not too steep, not too flat.

FRANCE

Segovia
Madrid

SPAIN

✎ A different use for the arch, to support a road over a river; we call it a bridge!

The Romans used the arch
to make strong bridges over rushing rivers.
With these bridges,
Rome improved transportation
and connected the great empire together.

✎ The perfect form of the arch is so strong that even rushing water and flood do not wash it away.

The Roman arch
was shaped like
a semicircle, a half-circle.

The Romans used rows of arches
to build the walls of great coliseums
where gladiators fought
in front of roaring crowds.

See how the arches are semicircles?

✎ Arch after arch, all perfect, all alike. Stones make arches, and circles of arches make a coliseum.

Some of the arches
the Romans built are huge.
They rise high in the air,
and support a massive weight of stone.

Arches allowed the Romans to build
great public buildings,
and the arch is so strong a form
that many of these buildings
are still standing,
almost 2,000 years
after the Roman Empire fell.

✎ Talk about what
2,000 years means.
Develop a deep feeling
about how long ago
Rome was, compared
to 1776.

✎ Develop a sense of scale here. Let students think about how high this building was. Note still another use of the arch.

When the Romans
wanted to honor a hero,
they would sometimes build a
magnificent ornamental arch,
such as the one at right,
dedicated to emperor Constantine,
who won a great battle in 315 A.D.

✎ Tell students it was Constantine who made Christianity the official religion of the Roman Empire.

The head of a bust of Constantine.

✎ Ask students how long they think it took to make this great arch an index of its importance to the people.

✎ Observe that our language, alphabet, legal systems, and even architecture have been modeled on the Romans examples.

Great Roman arches still inspire
modern architects.

The Roman-style arch in Washington Square,
which is in New York City's
Greenwich Village,
was built in 1889 to honor
the centennial of George Washington's
inauguration as president
of the United States.

✎ Talk about the word *centennial*, a one-hundred-year anniversary.

ARCADE

A row of arches
is an **arcade**.
The Romans used
arcades in buildings,
and they also
used stacked arcades,
one on top of another,
to construct the great
aqueducts that carried
water to the city.

✎ Still another use of the arch. One strong element, used creatively in so many different ways.

The Roman aqueduct in Segovia, Spain, uses stacks of arcades to rise high into the air.

✎ The aqueduct in Segovia is especially beautiful. It is a reminder that the Romans occupied Spain, resulting eventually in Spanish.

THE PONT DU GARD

This aqueduct is called the Pont du Gard.
It is near Nimes, France.
It crosses the Gard River and is much
more massive than the aqueduct
in Segovia.

✎ The Pont du Gard is massive and heavy, unlike the aqueduct in Segovia. It shows how powerful arches can be, to hold up such immense weight.

The Pont du Gard is made of three stacks of arcades, with a water channel on top.

900 feet long and more than 50 meters high,
the Pont du Gard was begun in 19 B.C.
during the reign of Augustus,
and finished a century later,
during the reign of Emperor Trajan.
Trajan ruled from 98 to 117 A.D.

✎ The headline font in this book is called TRAJAN. It is a Roman all-caps font, inspired by a lettering style used during the Roman empire.

The arch
was strong,
but it also gave
Roman
buildings
grace and
beauty.

✎ The stone work and curves of the arches are especially beautiful in shadow. Here the arches are used in the interior of a building.

Even today,
some of the
Roman ruins
are among
the most
beautiful
designs
in the world.

✎ Roman architecture is like Leggos; a few simple forms like arches and columns, combined in thousands of different ways.

But the gifts of Rome
to modern civilization
include more than the arch
or Roman architecture.

From the Romans,
we also received important ideas
about law and government,
classics of literature,
and perhaps most important,
language.

✎ It is almost impossible to believe that the Romans built such magnificent structures 2,000 years ago. Will our buildings be standing in 4010?

ROMAN ROCKS, ROMAN WORDS

✎ The Romans borrowed the word *amphitheater* from the Greeks. Amphi means both; an amphitheater curves around both sides of the audience.

Just as many arches that the Romans built
more than 2,000 years ago still stand,
so many of the words and parts of words
that the Romans spoke are still spoken.
Even today, we can see familiar words
carved in ancient Roman stones.

LATIN · A BRIDGE TO THE PAST

Latin, the language of the Romans,
is the rock that many modern languages—
including English, Spanish, and others—build on.
In part, English and Spanish are made of Latin,
and so they are a word-bridge to the distant past.

STEMS AND STONES

Just as the Romans put stones
together to make an arch,
so they put parts of words together
to make words.

These word parts, which we call **stems**,
join together to make words.
If we add the stem **pre**,
which means before, to the stem **dict**,
we get the word **predict**.

✎ Here is the guiding metaphor of this book, that stems make words like stones make arches. Things are made of pieces.

PRE · DICT
PREDICT

This makes sense! **Pre** means before,
and **dict** means say.
To **predict** is to say something
is going to happen, *before* it does.

Pre is an important stem.
We find the Latin **pre**
in lots of English words, such as **pre**view,
predict, **pre**vent, **pre**school, **pre**cede, **pre**pare,
and even **pre**position.

✎ This is an example
to establish the
concept of stems. The
stem lessons come
later.

There are
lots and lots
of Latin stems
like **pre**,
that we use
to build words,
both in English
and in other
modern languages,
such as Spanish.

✎ This text will not
present all of the stems
in the masonry. It is a
graphic image to make
the point of how stems
combine to make
something big.

GOOD RELATIVES

English also has words from other sources such as Greek.

By comparing the stems in words
from Latin, English, and Spanish,
we can see that
the two modern languages
are relatives,
which have both descended
from Latin,
their common
ancient source.

✎ There are other romance languages other than Spanish, but it is important to give Spanish greater emphasis than ever before.

LATIN	ENGLISH	SPANISH
praeparare	prepare	preparar
aquaeductus	aqueduct	acueducto
semestris	semester	semestre
semicirculus	semicircular	semicircular
magnanimus	magnanimous	magnánimo
magnitudo	magnitude	magnitud
amphitheatrum	amphitheater	anfiteatro
spectaculum	spectacular	espectaculo
spectrum	specter	espectro
reiterarare	reiterate	reiterar
repetere	repeat	repetir
mediterraneus	mediterranean	mediterráneo
medius	medium	mediano
subterraneus	subterranean	subterráneo

✎ Spend some time looking over these common elements with students, until they get a feel for how closely the languages are related.

AQUAEDUCTUS
Latin

AQUEDUCT
English

ACUEDUCTO
Spanish

In all three languages,
the stem **aqua** means water,
and **duct** means lead.
The aqueduct led the water to Rome.

Made of arcades of arches,
the aqueducts could cross rivers
and span valleys,
bringing cold, fresh water
down a channel at the top of the aqueduct.

✎ Keep emphasizing that English and Spanish are both expressing modern variations of the ancient Latin that the Romans spoke.

The lead-lined water channel was at the top of the aqueduct.

Water flowed down a channel lined with lead, to prevent leaking

✎ The aqueduct was built to duct the aqua, and it worked. It was a massive project, but the Romans needed fresh water badly.

Why did the Romans go to so much trouble to bring water down from the mountains? The Romans did not have pumps, that would let them raise lots of water from underground wells, but they did have gravity, that would move water downhill, from the lakes and rivers high above Rome and their other cities. Sometimes the water was dozens of miles from the city, and the Romans had to build an aqueduct the whole way, creating a gradual slope for miles. The water ran in a channel at the top of the aqueduct, which was lined with lead to prevent leaks. When the engineers came to a steep river valley, they used tiers of arches to raise their aqueduct high into the air. This let the water at the top continue its gentle downhill flow. Today, now that we have underground pipes and large pumps that move water to our cities, we no longer need to build aqueducts, but many of the beautiful aqueducts built by the Romans still stand as a testament to their ancient engineering genius.

GREAT LATIN STEMS

Because Latin stems
are so important to the English language,
we will take a close look
at some of the best stems.

Each one has
its own important meaning.

The stems fit together to make words,
like stones fit together to build an arch.

✎ Now that we have prepared the historical basis for it, we begin the vocabulary focus of the book. We want students to have a historical perspective.

In the Roman
aqueducts,
the same arch
form was
repeated,
over and
over again.

✎ There are simple
structures in nature,
such as carbon atoms,
that are reiterated in
thousands of ways to
generate life forms.
The arch is like that.

RE

AGAIN

Re means again.

We find Rome's **re** in English words, we do;
such as **re**peat, **re**turn, **re**verse, **re**view,
revise, **re**flect, **re**call, **re**do,
rehearse, **re**spect, and even **re**new.

✎ Always linger over this first page, thinking about how the stem works in some of the words, and asking the students to think of other examples.

When the arches fall to ruin,
we **re**build them, by **re**newing
them again.

✎ Much of the text is poetry or semipoetic, just to make it more fun. This page extends the exposure to example words. Discuss meanings.

Once upon a time,
there was a small stem named Re.
Re saw Sub crouching under an arch,
and Sub said, "Hi!"
"Hi, hi, hi!" said Re.
Sub laughed, in his low voice,
then Re laughed and laughed and laughed.
Sub asked Re,
"Do you remember why
arches are strong, or should I review?"
"I recall," said Re, "I recall."
"Good," said Sub, with new respect.
Then, they looked up
at the keystone.

✎ The story in each list personifies the stems, and gives them characters that deepen their meanings. Always discuss why each stem behaves as it does.

A RE CLOSEUP

RESPECT

RE · SPECT

Respect, to admire, is a wonderful word,
containing **re**, again, and **spect**, look.
When we learn to **re**spect someone,
we look at that person again,
in a new way!

✎ The closeup puts one example word in the spotlight. Combine this with looking up the word in the dictionary, and thoroughly discuss the word.

RE IN SPANISH

Just as **re** is an important stem in English,
it is also important in Spanish.
Here is a Spanish **re** word:

repetir, to repeat

Yo   *quiero*   **re***petir*   *la*   *palabra.*
I   want   to repeat   the   word.

✎ The key here is the stem, and the idea that it inhabits BOTH languages and means the same in both. English and Spanish are connected.

A RE POEM

When Flea saw Skin again,
his feelings were **re**newed.
He stalled, **re**viewed, **re**called
it all, and **re**turned to his food!

See if you can write
a poem of four lines,
using lots of **re** words,
and even some rhymes.
It is ok if your poem is funny!

✎ The poem activity
teaches poetic
technique and gives
students experience
using stem words.
They will have to think
about the words.

When we remember, we return in our minds!

A RE SIMILE

Here is something fun to do.
Pick a **re** word, and then you
compare it to something very different:

A memory IS LIKE a return.

This kind of comparison
is called a simile (SIM ih lee).
Write your own simile, and explain it!

✎ The simile activity teaches students about similes, encourages synthesis via comparison, and immerses students in example words.

An
aqueduct
is
like
respect.

✎ When we see an
aqueduct, we turn and
look at it again, it is so
impressive. Respect is
like that; we look at the
person again, with new
admiration.

To wit means for example, or that is.

SUB

UNDER

Sub means under.

We find **sub** in English words, to wit: **sub**tract, **sub**lime, **sub**scribe, **sub**mit, **sub**marine, and **sub**urb; then we get **sub**stitute, **sub**soil, and **sub**way—they fit!

✎ Keep emphasizing the fact that many words make sense, that they are not just accidental sequences of sounds or letters, but are logical.

In **sub**urb's arches, columns stand;
holding up the top, as planned.
Ancient Romans used to toil,
building columns on **sub**soil.

✎ In this painting, you can see both the arches and the columns that support them. The columns would be built on solid subsoil below.

Sub was crawling around, down low,
and here came Re again.
"Ohhhowwww," moaned Sub.
Re started, then stopped, then started,
then stopped. "Sub? Sub?" Re asked.
"Down here," groaned Sub, "Lower."
Re leaned over and peeked
under the lowest arch,
and looked again.
"I see you, I see you!" Re said.
"Ohhhh," moaned Sub,
and he burrowed down in the soil,
only his eyes showing.

✎ Since *sub* means under, Sub is always down low and speaking in low moans and tones, and is often emotionally down, as well!

A SUB CLOSEUP

SUBURB

SUB · URB

Sub means under, and **urb** means city.

A city is an urban place,
but gathered close around
are **sub**urbs where the people live
and travel into town.

✎ The emphasis in this book is on the great, main stems that are in dozens or hundreds of words. We have featured the easiest example words.

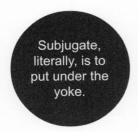
Subjugate, literally, is to put under the yoke.

SUB IN SPANISH

Just as **sub** is important in English,
it is also important in Spanish.
Here is a Spanish **sub** word:

subyugar, to subjugate
(to subjugate is to conquer or defeat)

Caesar	***sub**yugó*	*las*	*tribus*	*de Gaul.*
Caesar	subjugated	the	tribes	of Gaul.

✎ Remind students that Gaul is now France, and that Caesar led the Roman legions north from Rome into Gaul. Discuss *subjugate*.

A SUB POEM

Sub went underneath the top
of the soil, to help the crop
grow green; down he toiled—
deep in **sub**terranean Roman **sub**soil!

See if you can write
your own poem of four lines,
using lots of **sub** words,
and even some rhymes.
It is ok if your poem is funny!

✎ You can point out
that *sub* means under
and *terr* means land,
so *subterranean*
means underground.

A SUB SIMILE

Let's write another simile,
just to see if we can think cleverly:

A submarine IS LIKE a mole.

Remember, this kind of comparison
is called a simile (SIM ih lee).
Write your own **sub** simile,
and explain it.

✎ The submarine goes under the sea, as the mole borrows under the land.

$$\begin{array}{r} 4 \\ -\ 1 \\ \hline 3 \end{array}$$

To
subtract
is like
pulling
one stone
from
an
arch.

✎ *Sub* means under, and *tract* means pull. We subtract by pulling one or more down out of the total. The word depicts subtraction, graphically.

DE

DOWN

De means down.

We find **de** in English words, you see,
like **de**scend, **de**posit, and **de**bris,
decay, **de**cide, and then **de**crease,
define, **de**pend, **de**scribe, easy!

✎ Use these words in sentences, and explain each word. You might like to use these words as a lesson for the dictionary.

When our old buildings **de**cay,
they **de**scend unto the clay,
and there, their **de**bris may stay!

✎ IMAGINATION:
Ask students to
imagine the life that
once took place when
Romans lived here.
 Discuss *there* and
their.

De went down to find Re and Sub.
She leaned down and helped Sub up,
and called for Re. "Re?" she called.
"Here, here here!" cried Re,
and he ran and ran to the spot.
"What's up, Sub?" asked Re,
"You look down. Down. Down."
"Ohhhh," said Sub, "I'm just low."
De looked down at her two buddies.
"Perk up, Sub," she said, and
reached down to pat his back.
"Right, Re?" De asked.
"Right, right. Right," said Re.

✎ ANALYSIS: Re repeats everything. The stems stay in character. Ask the students to explain why the stems act as they do.

A DE CLOSEUP

DESCRIBE

DE · SCRIB

Describe is a **de**scriptive word;
it recalls the moment when we
write, **scrib**, down, **de**, what something is like.
Of course, we don't always write
our **de**scriptions down,
but that is the image in the word!

✎ A micropoem: the word *describe* is like a little picture of someone writing down; lots of words are like this; they have little pictures in them.

DE IN SPANISH

Just as **de** is an important stem in English,
it is also important in Spanish.
Here is a Spanish **de** word:

definir, to define

Necesito	**de**finir	*mis*	*metas.*
I need	to define	my	goals.

✎ Like *define*, *definir* has *de* and then *fin* (end, limit). Many Spanish and English words have identical stems, in the identical order!

A DE POEM

The hawk **de**scended, with good luck,
landing on the aqueduct,
depositing upon the stone,
debris he'd gathered, ere he had flown.

See if you can write
a poem of four lines,
using lots of **de** words,
and even some rhymes.
It is ok if your poem is funny!

✎ Trying to write a short poem using stem words will cause students to think hard about the words. Invite them to feature more than one stem!

A DE SIMILE

Now it's time for a simile with de;
do your best, and we will see:

A decrease IS LIKE a leak.

Write your own **de** simile,
and explain it!

✎ After the students invent their own similes, either alone or in groups, go over them together and enjoy them. Let students explain.

A
descent
is
like
a
slide.

✎ A magnificent
image of the aqueduct.
We can imagine the
water sliding downhill
as it pours through the
carefully descending
slope of the aqueduct.

EX

OUT

Ex means out.

We find **ex** often now, I think:
exit, **ex**tend, **ex**pand, **ex**tinct,
extract, **ex**plode, **ex**pose,
explore, **ex**port, **ex**cept—all those.

✎ You could ask students to count how many *ex* words they find in a college-level dictionary. They will then see that this is only a tiny sample.

If you want the **ex**it, out,
extend your mind, **ex**pand your snout!
Explore the arches, that's the route.

✎ In order to enjoy words fully, look up their etymologies in a good dictionary. What does the part after the *ex* mean?

Thinking she was all alone,
Ex looked around,
trying to find the way out.
"Is anybody here?" Ex called.
"Nope," came Sub's voice, from under a rock.
"Not me, not me, not me," came Re's voice,
from somewhere close.
"I'm not here," came De's voice,
in a descending tone.
Then, she saw the arch,
and went through it,
out into the sun.

✎ By now, students should be able to write their own little stem stories, in which they personify the stems by linking behavior with definition.

AN EX CLOSEUP

EXPORT

EX · PORT

Stems are inherently interdisciplinary; Explore paths.

Export is a very good word;
to **ex**port a product
is to sell it abroad,
to carry, **port**, it out, **ex**,
of the country.

✎ Discuss the difference between exports and imports.

EX IN SPANISH

Just as *ex* is an **ex**cellent stem in English,
it is also **ex**ceptional in Spanish.
Here is a Spanish *ex* word:

exceder, to define

¿*Es*		*bueno*	*exceder*	*los*	*límites?*
Is	(it)	good	to exceed	the	limits?

✎ A great short project: spend a few days studying and researching the history of the Romans in Spain.

AN EX POEM

These arches, since the day they rose,
have been unto the sun **ex**posed,
Extending up into the air,
to bring fresh water down from there.

See if you can write
a poem of four lines,
using lots of **ex** words,
and even some rhymes.
It is ok if your poem is funny!

✎ Students can use any rhyme scheme they like. Or they can just search for words that sound similar, and put them anywhere in the lines.

✎ The aqueduct in Segovia, Spain, is among the most magnificent remnants of ancient Rome.

AN EX SIMILE

Now it's time for a simile with **ex**;
about an out, as we expect:

An explosion IS LIKE a hooray.

Write your own **ex** simile,
and explain it!

✎ Discuss with
students, In what way
is an explosion like a
hooray? How many
ways is it like a
hooray?

An
extending
column
in an
aqueduct
is like
an
expansive
dream.

✎ An expansive
dream would be one
that extends way out,
with lots of detail and
depth, just as this
aqueduct extends so
high into the sky.

In most words, *spec* has a *t* added.

SPEC

LOOK

Spec means look.

Of **spec** our language is so full:
in**spec**t, re**spec**t, and **spec**tacle...
spectacular and **spec**trum too,
and **spec**tres haunt Rome's ruins...Boo!

✎ Yes, a spectre is a ghost, but we don't mean that there are really ghosts; it is just a fantasy that makes a fun sentence.

A **spec**tacle is quite a sight,
when gladiators join the fight;
now, Roman **spec**tres haunt the site.
We see 'em in the Coliseum.

✎ There are spectacles we watch, and spectacles we watch with glasses! Talk about the difference.

Spec looked here,

and spec looked there.

He looked, well, really,

everywhere.

But Ex was out,

and Sub was under,

and Re had done it again—no wonder.

De was down, and wouldn't play,

so Spec just passed the day away,

looking,

we suspect.

Project:
Draw the stem characters.
What colors are they? Why?

✎ The students could write a short play, with each student acting out the role of a stem. They could perform the play for their friends.

76

A SPEC CLOSEUP

INSPECT

IN · SPEC

Let us inspect this word, *inspect*.
It uses the stem **in**, which means in!
And it also uses **spec**, look.
To **inspec**t is to look into something,
to consider it very carefully.

✎ The spec words are particularly vivid and fascinating; looking at things is such a central part of human life.

SPEC IN SPANISH

Spec is an important stem in English,
and it is also part of Spanish.
Here is a Spanish *spec* word:

sospechar, to suspect

Sospecho	*que*	*el*	*hombre*	*tiene*	*muchos*	*libros*.
I suspect	that	the	man	has	many	books.

✎ We want to keep reinforcing the links between English and Spanish; this leads to a sense of the importance of knowing Spanish and being bilingual.

A SPEC POEM

The **spec**tacles in Roman times
were witnessed by re**spec**tful lines
of Roman **spec**tators who thought
that gladiators bravely fought.

See if you can write
a poem of four lines,
using lots of **spec** words,
and even some rhymes.
It is ok if your poem is funny!

✎ We want to push the sense of play in the poem assignment; let students work in small groups so they can talk about words and rhymes.

A SPEC SIMILE

In each case, we see a sequence of pretty colors.

Now it's time for a simile with **spec**;
and it should be something to look at:

A spectrum IS LIKE a box of crayons.

Write your own **spec** simile,
and explain it!

✎ Spectrum is a big word, but one easily taught. Students will like the colors of the spectrum and its similarity to crayons.

Seeing
a
spectacular
view
through
an arch,
is like
thinking
hard
about
one
friend.

✎ Through the arch,
we see a captivating
landscape; it holds us,
like the vision of a
friend we are thinking
hard about.

A STEM STORY

✎ This story should be read slowly, a game to find every single stem and notice the word it is in. Discuss the meaning of each sentence.

Cold mountain water descended through the channel at the top of the aqueduct, as the architect had repeatedly predicted it would. Unprepared, the people had not believed the architect, when he had described how the aqueduct, with its high arcades of arches, would conduct the water down. Now, thirsty Romans gathered in city squares to inspect the spectacle: fresh water, pouring from spouts. A miracle. Water would not have to be transported. The previously used subterranean wells, with their foul smell, would not be rebuilt. The aqueduct system would be expanded and extended. With ceremony, they inscribed the architect's name on a stone. In the distance the spectacular sea rolled, an aquamarine blue, and whitecaps made spots on its surface.

REVIEW

✎ Review and quiz the students on the stems on these two pages. Help them use the example words in sentences. Explain the definitions to them.

FEATURE STEMS	CLOSEUP WORDS
RE · AGAIN	RESPECT · TO ADMIRE
SUB · UNDER	SUBURB · NEIGHBORHOODS NEAR A CITY
DE · DOWN	DESCRIBE · TO PORTRAY IN WORDS
EX · OUT	EXPORT · TO SELL TO A FOREIGN COUNTRY
SPEC · LOOK	INSPECT · TO EXAMINE SOMETHING

OTHER STEMS WE HAVE NOTICED

✎ These stems have been glimpsed along the way, and some will later be feature stems.
✎ Have the students write a little story, using lots of stem words.

STEM	A GOOD EXAMPLE WORD
IN · IN	INSCRIBE · TO WRITE IN
DUCT · LEAD	AQUEDUCT · STRUCTURE THAT BRINGS WATER
PRE · BEFORE	PREDICT · TO SAY SOMETHING WILL HAPPEN

URB · CITY	URBAN · OF THE CITY
DICT · SAY	DICTIONARY · A BOOK ABOUT WORDS
SCRIB · WRITE	SCRIBE · A PERSON WHO WRITES
AQUA · WATER	AQUATIC · OF THE WATER
PORT · CARRY	TRANSPORT · TO MOVE

QUESTIONS TO THINK ABOUT

FOR WHICH STEM CAN YOU THINK OF THE MOST EXAMPLE WORDS?

WHICH EXAMPLE WORD IS MOST LIKE A PICTURE? WHY?

WHICH EXAMPLE WORD MAKES THE MOST SENSE? WHY?

WHICH STEM IS YOUR FAVORITE? WHY?

WHICH NEW WORD ARE YOU LIKELY TO USE? EXPLAIN.

CAN YOU THINK OF YOUR OWN EXAMPLE WORDS FOR THESE STEMS?
WHAT ARE THEY?

SUPER

OVER

Super means over.

A **super**b stem is this one, here;
superior to many, dear.
When **super**stitions cloud your eyes,
this stem will help you realize
how **super**ficial are those ideas!

✎ Even with these basic stems, many of the example words are advanced. Use your own judgment about which words to focus on.

Roman architects, **super**b,
built their arches, spoke their words,
supervising Roman workers here,
urging them to do **super**ior
work.

✎ Sometimes, as with the word *superb*, only one letter is added to a stem to make it a word. In fact, *super* is itself a word.

Super saw Sub, who was really down.
"Hey, Subby!" giggled Super,
"Isn't this a great day! Wow!"
"You're sure up," groaned Sub.
"Yep, old Subby" beamed Super,
"Where's the gang?"
"O," moaned Sub,
"Re's in his loop,
De's in her slump,
Ex is outa here,
and Spec looks out for himself."
"Not to worry!" cried Super,
"Everything's gonna be all right!"
"Right," said Sub,
and crawled back under the arch.

✎ *Super* means over, and so Super here is happy and emotionally high up. Sub and De are down, as usual.

Words like *over* and *cover* are called eye-rhyme!

A SUPER CLOSEUP

SUPERVISE

SUPER · VIS

Supervise is quite a word,
with **super**, over—as you have heard;
and **vis** (like vision), which means look.
(Vis and Spec could write a book.)
To **super**vise is watching over
those who need protection's cover.

✎ *Supervise* is so visual; you can just see someone looking over others. A micropoem. Emphasize how our words have these little hidden poems in them.

SUPER IN SPANISH

Super is an important stem in English,
and it is also part of Spanish.
Here is a Spanish *super* word:

superar, to overcome

Es	*importante*	***super****ar*	*nuestros*	*probemas*.
It is	important	to overcome	our	problems.

✎ Discuss the bilingual signs and packing instructions students see, and discuss why this is increasing so rapidly.

A SUPER POEM

A **super**stitious thing to think
(and **super**ficial) is that drinking
water upside down
makes **super**natural beings frown.

See if you can write
a poem of four lines,
using lots of **super** words,
and even some rhymes.
It is ok if your poem is funny!

✎ The poem is just a joke, not a declaration that there are really supernatural beings, such as the students see in cartoons or movies.

A SUPER SIMILE

A simile with **super** must be over-done;
see if you can think of one:

A superstition IS LIKE falling for a trick.

Write your own **super** simile,
and explain it!

✎ Yes, superstitions are unfounded and often odd beliefs that persist in spite of contradicting evidence; they trick us.

The
superior
strength
of the
arch
is like
a
waterfall
in a
photograph.

✎ In a photo, the falling water is stopped, frozen in place like the cascading stone in this beautiful aqueduct. Both endure in time.

PRE

BEFORE

Pre means before.

Prepare yourself for this good stem,
it **pre**cedes others, like the limb
precedes the leaves, as you
predict and **pre**view
what comes when, don't you?

✎ *Pre* is one of the most important stems; it is present in hundreds and hundreds of words. Why? Time is a big part of being human.

Forthwith means immediately.

The architect had to **pre**dict
the weight of stones—a clever trick;
he then **pre**pared the arches' width,
and **pre**viewed his design, forthwith.

✎ It is good to have the students think about the architect. Arches are human creations, not just abstract geometrical forms.

Pre went first, and helped Sub
crawl under the arch, down where De was
waiting. Next, Ex came out,
with Spec looking about to make sure
the coast was clear.
Super peeked over the arch,
and Re just did it his own way,
over and over again.
You know him.
Away they went, preceded by Pre,
Ex exiting out, De and Sub
covering the low ground,
Spec looking around,
and Re hopping along behind —
boing, boing, boing.
From here, we lost sight of Pre first.

Project:
Get clay, and
make stem
characters.

✎ Ask the students
who their favorite stem
character is, and why.
If they had to interview
one, which one would
it be?

A PRE CLOSEUP

PRECEDE

PRE · CEDE

Precede means to go before,
with **pre**, before (but there is more).
See, **cede** means go,
and you should know,
that Rome **pre**ceded all we know.

✎ Ask the kids to give other examples of things that preceded other things, or of things that MUST precede other things.

PRE IN SPANISH

Pre is an important stem in English,
and it is also part of Spanish.
Here is a Spanish *pre* word:

preceder, to go before

El	*viento*	***pre****cede*	*a la*	*tormenta.*
The	wind	goes before	the	storm.

✎ Here, the Spanish word is almost exactly the same as the English word. In the sentence, it is pronounced pray-SAY-day.

A PRE POEM

Roman sages **pre**viewed omens
to **pre**dict their future scares;
Roman citizens were showing
how they **pre**ferred to **pre**pare.

See if you can write
a poem of four lines,
using lots of **pre** words,
and even some rhymes.
It is ok if your poem is funny!

✎ Their rhymes can be at the ends of the lines (end rhyme), or can be between words inside the lines (internal rhyme).

A PRE SIMILE

To make a simile with **pre**,
prepare your idea carefully.

A preview IS LIKE distant thunder.

Write your own **pre** simile,
and explain it!

✎ A preview gives us
an advance indication
of what is to come, just
as the sound of distant
thunder does.

Predicting
the
future
is like
trying
to see
the
distance.

✎ In this painting, we see a nice example of perspective narrowing as the objects are more and more distant. The more distant, the harder to see.

Point out that *post* is the opposite of *pre*.

POST

AFTER

Post means after.

We can't for long **post**pone this stem;
since ***post meridiem*** is called *p.m.*
And as a **post**script we will reason:
P.S.: The games are over by the **post**season.

✎ Here is a great opportunity to teach about *p.m.* and *P.S. Post* is another important stem, though many of its example words are advanced.

The arch was in part a message to posterity.

Our **post**erity come after us,
and carry on our names and such,
we call them our *descendents*, too,
and hope they honor what we do.

✎ Here you can discuss what synonyms are, and introduce a big word (*posterity*) that is easy when you understand it.

The whole gang got organized.
Pre went first, and Post went last.
Sub got on the bottom,
and Super got on the top.
De got down, and Ex went out,
Spec looked all about,
and Re just kept it up, and wouldn't quit,
even when they asked him to.
What a kidder.
At the end, Post had to make Re stop it.
Re didn't budge.
"Move along," said Post, "After you."
"Okay, okay, okay!" said Re.
Post waited a second,
and then followed the others.

✎ Point out that many of these stems show relationships; i.e., *post* means something comes after something else.

104

A POST CLOSEUP

POSTPONE

POST · PON

Postpone means to put after,
since **post** means after and **pon** means put,
so before you burst into loud laughter,
we've told you what is what!

In Spanish the verb *poner* means to put. *Pon* is a form of *pos*, as in *deposit*, *impose*, and *compose*.

POST IN SPANISH

Post is an important stem in English,
and it is also part of Spanish.
Here is a Spanish ***post*** word:

posteridad, posterity
Our posterity are our descendents.

*Necesitamos   pensar   en   nuestra   **post**eridad.*
We need   to think   of   our   posterity.

> ✎ More evidence that Spanish is part of our family; *posteridad* and *posterity* are almost identical. Our languages have deep connections.

A POST POEM

The pretest is the early check
to see what we don't know;
the **post**test helps us to inspect
if we have learned—Uh oh!

See if you can write
a poem of four lines,
using lots of **post** words,
and even some rhymes.
It is ok if your poem is funny!

✎ Lines 1 and 3 have near rhyme, and lines 2 and 4 have true rhyme.

A POST SIMILE

Your ideas have to be uncrossed
to make a simile with **post**.

A postscript IS LIKE a small dessert.

Write your own **post** simile,
and explain it!

✎ The P.S. of a letter
is just a small point
added after the letter,
as the dessert comes
after the main meal.

Our
posterity
are
like
echoes.

✎ Our descendents
will reflect influences
that come from our
lives; things we begin
will play out in future
generations, like fading
echoes.

PORT

CARRY

Port means carry.

The Romans used to ex**port** loads
trans**port**ing them along the roads,
and im**port** too, with equal ease
to all their Roman colonies.

✎ As time goes on,
kids will notice that
there are lots and lots
of *port* words. *Port* is a
major stem.

Barbarians from Gaul (now France)
re**port**ed to their tribes
that Roman legions' **port**able lances
gave them scary vibes!

✎ Time to note that places had different names in ancient times. Once, France was Gaul, which was attacked and conquered by Caesar.

"Hey, Port," cried Super, "Bring Re over here."
Port picked Re up, but Re cried,
"Put me down, put me down, put me down."
So Port put him down,
on top of Sub, who said
"Ooooff. Get offame, Re,"
and Re rolled onto De, who said
"Hey, get off!" and Re grabbed onto Ex,
who was on her way out, but Ex said,
"Let go, please!" and split, and so Re
bounded toward Post, who was at the back,
but Post said "Yikes! Leave me alone!"
so Re looked at Spec, who had been
watching the whole thing,
but Spec just stared him down.
"Ok," said Re, and Port picked him up again,
and transported him over there.

✎ Ask the students to write a short dialogue between any two stems; the dialogue must show the personalities of the stems.

A PORT CLOSEUP

TRANSPORT

TRANS · PORT

Transport means to move something a distance, since **trans** means across and **port** means carry; Julius Caesar trans**port**ed captives, for instance, back to Rome, which was very bad luck for them!

> ✎ You might tell the kids that Julius Caesar wrote a book, which we still read, about the Gallic Wars.

PORT IN SPANISH

Port is an important stem in English,
and it is also part of Spanish.
Here is a Spanish ***port*** word:

portador, carrier

*Voy   a   pagar   al   **port**ador   de   esta   carta.*
I'm going   to pay   the   carrier   of   this   letter.

✎ Another interesting connection: in Spanish *carta* is letter, and we remember the *Magna Carta* in English history.

A PORT POEM

Romans had to trans**port** stone
to build the aqueducts,
and **port**ers carried tools alone—
it's re**port**ed in the books!

See if you can write
a poem of four lines,
using lots of **port** words,
and even some rhymes.
It is ok if your poem is funny!

✎ Have the kids imagine all the things that had to be transported in order to build a great aqueduct: stone, food, tools...

A PORT SIMILE

To make a simile with **port**
you have to be a clever sort.

Transport IS LIKE a leaf on a stream.

Write your own **port** simile,
and explain it!

✎ We see the leaf
carried along on the
stream, just like we
see goods carried
along a road by the
means of transport.

116

A
ruin
is like
a
re**port**
from
the
past.

✎ Like a written
report, a ruin gives us
facts from the distant
past. Either way, we
only know a limited
amount of the past.

Distort means away-twist! Good image!

DIS

AWAY

Dis means away.

You will not **dis**agree, we think,
that having a **dis**tracted mind can sink
the best intentions. To **dis**pute this
would be silly; to **dis**miss
it would **dis**tort—or yes—**dis**pose
of truth? Who knows?

✎ *Tract* in *distract* means pull; *put* in *dispute* means think; *pos* in *dispose* means *put*. In *dismiss*, *miss* means send.

118

The Romans now have **dis**appeared,
and Italy is there,
and Roman arches, as we feared,
are in some **dis**repair.

✎ These arches are in disrepair. Imagine a Roman citizen coming through the arch. The arch's state of repair has certainly gone away!

Dis was trying to sneak away.
He left Post in the back,
and De was too down to notice,
but Spec was watching and saw Dis leave,
as did Super, who had a good view
from over the arch.
Of course, out came Ex,
and Sub warned everyone with his low moan,
from somewhere under the arch.
Pre came after Dis first,
and Port hurried along, carrying Re,
whose "Stop it, stop it, stop it"
repeated across the fields.
They were too late.
Slowly, Dis made it.
He disappeared.

✎ The kids can each become a stem, work up a creative/funny costume, and give a little performance.

We also
see *tract*
in the word
tractor.

A DIS CLOSEUP

DISTRACT

DIS · TRACT

To be **distracted**, as you know,
is to lose your attention, yes, in full;
for **dis** means away, and **tract** means pull—
but we're too **dis**tracted to listen now.

✎ *Tract* means pull,
so the word *distract* is
a great image of being
pulled away! Many
words are almost like
cartoons, once you
understand them.

DIS IN SPANISH

Dis is an important stem in English,
and it is also part of Spanish.
Here is a Spanish *dis* word:

distancia, distance

Yo	*veo*	*la*	*ciudad*	*en*	*la*	***dis**tancia*.
I	see	the	city	in	the	distance.

A DIS POEM

Though Rome has **dis**appeared today,
its words have been **dis**persed.
Like **dis**tant poems that we say,
distributed in verse.

See if you can write
a poem of four lines,
using lots of **dis** words,
and even some rhymes.
It is ok if your poem is funny!

✎ There are pages
and pages of *dis* words
in the dictionary. Let
students look for
others, such as
disgrace, that they
know.

A DIS SIMILE

The explanations are key; the reasons.

To make a simile with **dis**
—don't **dis**agree—it looks like this:

An arch in a ruin IS LIKE a distant sound.

Write your own **dis** simile,
and explain it!

✎ A distant sound is just one part of the whole sound; only a piece comes to us, like an arch is just one piece in a ruin, one piece that we see.

Long
shadows
are like
distracted
minds.

✎ The long shadows
are pulled way out by
the light, just as the
mind is pulled away by
a distraction.

REVIEW

FEATURED LATIN STEMS

DE · DOWN

EX · OUT

RE · AGAIN

SPEC · LOOK

SUB · UNDER

SUPER · OVER

PRE · BEFORE

POST · AFTER

PORT · CARRY

DIS · AWAY

OTHER STEMS WE HAVE NOTICED

STEM	A GOOD EXAMPLE WORD
IN · IN	INSCRIBE · TO WRITE IN
DUCT · LEAD	AQUEDUCT · STRUCTURE THAT BRINGS WATER
URB · CITY	URBAN · OF THE CITY
DICT · SAY	DICTIONARY · A BOOK ABOUT WORDS
SCRIB · WRITE	SCRIBE · A PERSON WHO WRITES
AQUA · WATER	AQUATIC · OF THE WATER
VIS - LOOK	VISION - THE SENSE OF SIGHT
CEDE - GO	PRECEDE - TO GO BEFORE
PON - PUT	POSTPONE - TO DELAY
TRANS - ACROSS	TRANSPORT - TO MOVE SOMETHING A DISTANCE
TRACT - PULL	DISTRACT - TO HAVE YOUR ATTENTION PULLED AWAY

THE SECRET OF WORDS

Now that we have learned important Latin stems, let's think about what we know. The English we speak is not new; it is a modern descendent of ancient Latin, and is a close relative of Spanish, which is even more similar to Latin. English and Spanish share many things, so to learn either is to learn some of the other. Both languages give modern voice to the ancient Romans, who conquered most of the Mediterranean world more than 2,000 years ago. One of Rome's gifts to civilization is the Roman arch that has been important to architecture ever since.

Like stones in the arch, Latin stems combine to make many English words. The stems we have learned are only a beginning. There are many more. Each stem is part of dozens or even hundreds of English and Spanish words, and by knowing the stem, you now know a part of the meaning of the word and why the word is spelled the way it is. Stems make vocabulary easy, powerful, and fun. By learning these Latin stems, you have begun to understand who you are, and where important parts of your mind came from.

Teacher Resources

A FOCUSED GOAL

The goal of this book is, in the most profound way, to give elementary kids the right vocabulary start. We want students to know, from their earliest thinking, that their world is not new, and that they did not come from nowhere. The English they speak, though it has a variety of sources, is in great part a linguistic ruin of Latin. Our minds were born, more than we realize, in Rome. It is the Latin-based words that are the nucleus of successful professional English, and it is the Latin-based words that dominate the classic words of English-language literature. These thousands of Latin-based English words, as if by a miracle, are built primarily with a few dozen easily learned stems, reused in myriad combinations, like children's blocks. By learning the stems, students discover a clicking vocabulary construction set that shows them how thousands of words are just recombinations of dozens of stems. And beyond just learning what words mean, students discover that spellings are usually logical, and that there is a secret poetry inside English words that is only visible if you know the stems. Stems let students begin their intellectual lives with the intellectual truth. Young students can start out as language insiders. Latin stems are power learning at its most beneficial.

The goal: to ground student vocabulary learning in its historical context of Rome, and to introduce ten Latin stems that are fundamental in English vocabulary.

TWO-PART DESIGN

In essence, *Building Language* has two parts, the historical background and the stem lessons. The first provides information about ancient Rome, focusing on Roman architecture and especially the arch, which is beautiful, intellectually enchanting, and which serves as a metaphor of how words are made of smaller pieces called stems. The book is even set in Roman type fonts, with Times Roman as the text and Trajan as the headline font, enhancing the aesthetic clarity. This is not, though, a history book, and it does not attempt to provide even a summary of Roman history. It introduces Rome as a backdrop to English vocabulary.

The second part provides ten lessons built around ten important Latin stems. In these lessons, a sense of play is enhanced with poetry and stories, and the lessons extend the interest in Rome and the arch through examples and references.

In the stem lessons, the close language relationship between English and Spanish is especially emphasized; Spanish has never been more important than it is today, and its kinship with English is woefully underappreciated. Since the stems that build English also build Spanish, this is a perfect opportunity to demonstrate the connected greatness of our two modern languages, and to provide knowledge that informs the study of both languages simultaneously.

~~AGE GRADED~~
REALISTIC VOCABULARY

Among the example words that appear in this book are some words that seem advanced, beyond the level of elementary children. First, this is inevitable in any examination of the Latin stems, since it is precisely the advanced stratum of English diction that stems create. But more importantly, it is imperative to elude the jaws of age-graded vocabulary assumptions. For decades, modern education has sunk, lower each year, under the tyranny of the assumption that students can not learn, and that only by providing the least possible content would any success be achieved. The spiral of dumbing-down textbooks has continued to the point that education has become a catastrophic void, a vast pessimism, with only the tiniest morsels of knowledge scattered about the gray topography. It must be the purpose of new educators to refuse these cowering assumptions, and to believe in children again, and to remember that every little child who can pronounce and understand a term like *Tyrannosaurus Rex* can certainly handle a term like *distort*. So if a lesson contains a word that is really new to the students, be not afraid. Teach them the word, talk and have fun, and discover how stems turn big words into child's play. Little kids *can* learn big words.

The truth is that children can learn much, much more than they are often asked to. Let's give them a challenging, realistic vocabulary.

✎ A distant sound is just one part of the whole sound; only a piece comes to us, like an arch is just one piece in a ruin, one piece that we see.

The arch was built as a message to posterity.

BOXES AND CIRCLES

The teacher's edition of *Building Language* employs boxes and circles on each page to provide talking points, explanations, suggestions for activities, and background comments to the teacher. The aim is to minimize how much the teacher has to flip to the back of the book to find an assignment or annotation. You have enough to do without having to flip. There is no crucial distinction between a box and a circle; if there was already a box, I put a circle the next time. It's prettier that way, and pretty matters.

THE ARCH

Part of the plan of this book is that if we are going to teach vocabulary, we may as well also use that opportunity to situate the vocabulary in the context of additional wonderful content. If we have to find example words and give example sentences, we may as well teach something important in the process. Fortunately, when it comes to teaching Latin stems, the opportunity is even more compelling; Rome looms dead ahead off the forward bow.

But in developing the concept of the book, we also saw the exciting chance to use Roman ruins as an opportunity to introduce architecture, and then the arch as a metaphor for how words are made of stems. This also presented a chance to make the book beautiful, and to use beautiful images to attract children to their own further study of Rome and of architecture. We should remember that beauty is intellectually important; it is a part of the central current of high intellectual life. Other reflections about the arch include:

• The arch is an amazingly flexible element. Here, it makes an arcade, there a doorway, a there a bridge, and there an aqueduct. It is eternally turning up in new locations, and is a wonderful proof of the human inventive power.

• The arch is a prototype for how smaller things make bigger things. This concept can be extended and explored with benefit. What are other examples of small things combining?

THE ROMANCE OF ETYMOLOGY

One of the goals of this program is to encourage the use of the dictionary, not only to look up the meaning of any word here, but to discover a path to the ancient origins of our modern words. It is important that students have access to a good dictionary that provides not just definitions and parts of speech, but also the Latin, Greek, or other origin of each word.

The challenge then falls upon us as educators to bring the adventure of etymology to light, and to bring a feeling of drama and exploration to each entry. This word comes from Rome! This word comes from the ancient Greeks! This word comes from a Native American civilization. This word comes from Spanish, and before that from Rome. Each time we look up a word in a good dictionary, we find a story, and if we don't read too fast, the story will speak up.

For classes that do have dictionaries, there are lots of opportunities for activities that will enhance this text:

- Look up the meaning of an example word.
- Look up lots of example words for a given stem.
- Look at all the examples in the whole dictionary of words beginning with a stem.
- Find your favorite stem word from the pages of the dictionary.

THE IMAGES

It is impossible to understand what the Romans achieved with stone unless you see it. The soaring grace of the Segovia aqueduct, as one example, leaves us dizzy with admiration. It is difficult to think of anything comparable that has been built since. And when we then learn that the aqueduct is not held together with cement, but only by gravity because the stones are so perfectly shaped and balanced, we sink into incredulity.

The images in this text are a kind of watered brushwork, faithful to the details but artistically enhanced to give the feeling of the soft art in children's books. They show the play of light among the stones, and suggest the contrasts of afternoons and mornings, and give a romantic feeling to the ruins that seem still so alive today, two millennia after they were built.

A SENSE OF TIME

Any look at the Roman empire, including our examination of the Roman fragments in English words, inevitably opens up our sense of time. In the United States, two hundred years seems like a long time; it extends almost to the founding of the nation in 1776. We forget that two individuals—each one living to be one hundred years old and the second one born on the day the first one died—would have lived through most of American history. Using this one-hundred-year life span as our unit of measure, we realize that five individuals could have lived through the entire history of the New World, from Columbus's discovery on.

Rome presents a different time scale entirely. It would take ten American histories to get back to the peak of the Roman empire. Columbus wasn't even born until 1451, a thousand years after Rome *fell*.

When we see these images of Roman ruins, and speak these fragments of Roman words, we are really traveling in time, in a manner for which American history offers no equivalent. So one of the tacit contents of this text is the concept of *time*.

As you move through the book, ask students subtle questions aimed at their sense of time: How long would it take for a building to become this ruin? What could have caused these walls to fall? Why are the parts that still stand, standing?

stem	definition	a variety of example words
de	down	descend, deposit, debris, decay, decide, decrease, define, describe
ex	out	exit, extend, expand, extinct, extract, explode, explore, export
re	again	repeat, return, reverse, review, revise, reflect, recall, redo, respect
spec	look	inspect, respect, spectacle, spectacular, spectrum, spectre
sub	under	subtract, subscribe, submit, submarine, suburb, subsoil, subway
super	over	superb, superior, superstition, superficial, supervise
pre	before	predict, preview, prevent, preschool, precede, prepare
post	after	postpone, post meridiem, postscript, postseason, posterity, posttest
port	carry	export, transport, import, porter, portable, report
dis	away	disagree, distract, dispute, dismiss, distort, disappear, distant
in	in	income, inscribe, inspect, include, indent, invade
duct	lead	conduct, introduction, product, reduction
urb	city	suburb, urban, urbane, urbanologist, urbanite
dict	say	predict, dictionary, dictate, dictator, malediction, contradict
scrib	write	prescribe, inscribe, scribe, scribble
aqua	water	aqueduct, aquarium, aquamarine
vis	look	vision, visor, revise, supervise
cede	go	precede, proceed, precedent, secede, antecedent, recede, intercede
pon	put	postpone (a variation of pos, put: position, deposit, impose, repose)
trans	across	transport, transfer, translate, transfusion, transcend
tract	pull	tractor, distract, retract, subtract, extract

QUIZ ONE

Define the stem that is in **bold**.

1. Water flowed down the channel in the aque**duct**. _____
2. The Romans **re**spected Constantine. _____
3. The wise man pre**dict**ed the fall of Rome. _____
4. The columns rested in the **sub**soil. _____
5. The architect in**spec**ted the arches. _____
6. The water **de**scended from the mountain. _____
7. Many goods were **ex**ported from Rome. _____
8. The emperor's words were **in**scribed in stone. _____
9. Stone was trans**port**ed for the arches. _____
10. The **scrib**e went with the emperor. _____
11. The **aque**duct crossed the river gorge. _____
12. The Roman legions **pre**ceded the general. _____
13. Rome was an ancient **urb**an location. _____

What word goes with this definition:

14. An official person who writes things down _____
15. To say something will happen before it does _____
16. An arched structure that carries water to the city _____
17. To sell things to a foreign country _____
18. Of the water; having to do with water _____
19. To move things a distance _____
20. The neighborhoods near a big city _____

QUIZ ONE

Define the stem that is in **bold**.

1.	Water flowed down the channel in the aque**duct**.	lead
2.	The Romans **re**spected Constantine.	again
3.	The wise man pre**dict**ed the fall of Rome.	say
4.	The columns rested in the **sub**soil.	under
5.	The architect in**spec**ted the arches.	look
6.	The water **de**scended from the mountain.	down
7.	Many goods were **ex**ported from Rome.	out
8.	The emperor's words were **in**scribed in stone.	in
9.	Stone was trans**port**ed for the arches.	carry
10.	The **scrib**e went with the emperor.	write
11.	The **aque**duct crossed the river gorge.	water
12.	The Roman legions **pre**ceded the general.	before
13.	Rome was an ancient **urb**an location.	city

What word goes with this definition:

14.	An official person who writes things down	scribe
15.	To say something will happen before it does	predict
16.	An arched structure that carries water to the city	aqueduct
17.	To sell things to a foreign country	export
18.	Of the water; having to do with water	aquatic
19.	To move things a distance	transport
20.	The neighborhoods near a big city	suburbs

QUIZ TWO

Define the stem that is in **bold**.

1. The words were in**scrib**ed in the stones._____
2. No one could pre**dict** what the barbarians would do. _____
3. The ocean was an **aqua**marine color. _____
4. There was a **spec**tacle in the colosseum._____
5. The **de**bris littered the ground beside the ruin. _____
6. The architect wanted to super**vise** the construction. _____
7. The scribe could **trans**late the barbarian language. _____
8. The fine was sub**tract**ed from the architect's fee._____
9. Stone was widely used in **urb**an architecture. _____
10. The drawings offered a **pre**view of the construction. _____
11. He had to post**pon**e building the aqueduct._____
12. The builders were **dis**tracted by the barbarian attacks. _____
13. The arch was **super**ior in strength to the beam. _____
14. The arch of Constantine was built for **post**erity._____
15. The materials had to pre**cede** the workers to the building site._____
16. The emperor personally came to **in**spect the progress on the aqueduct._____
17. The Romans im**port**ed many products from their colonies._____
18. The barbarians in Gaul would not **sub**mit to Caesar's rule. _____
19. Rome **ex**tended its power throughout the Mediterranean world. _____
20. The arch form was **re**peated the length of the aqueduct. _____

QUIZ TWO

Define the stem that is in **bold**.

1.	The words were in**scrib**ed in the stones.	write
2.	No one could pre**dict** what the barbarians would do.	say
3.	The ocean was an **aqua**marine color.	water
4.	There was a **spec**tacle in the colosseum.	look
5.	The **de**bris littered the ground beside the ruin.	down
6.	The architect wanted to super**vis**e the construction.	look
7.	The scribe could **trans**late the barbarian language.	across
8.	The fine was sub**tract**ed from the architect's fee.	pull
9.	Stone was widely used in **urb**an architecture.	city
10.	The drawings offered a **pre**view of the construction.	pre
11.	He had to post**pon**e building the aqueduct.	put
12.	The builders were **dis**tracted by the barbarian attacks.	away
13.	The arch was **super**ior in strength to the beam.	over
14.	The arch of Constantine was built for **post**erity.	after
15.	The materials had to pre**cede** the workers to the building site.	go
16.	The emperor personally came to **in**spect the progress on the aqueduct.	in
17.	The Romans im**port**ed many products from their colonies.	carry
18.	The barbarians in Gaul would not **sub**mit to Caesar's rule.	under
19.	Rome **ex**tended its power throughout the Mediterranean world.	out
20.	The arch form was **re**peated the length of the aqueduct.	again